COOPERATIVE IDEOLOGY

MAJOR STATEMENTS

The Author

Before marrying, Rita Rhodes was the full-time Secretary/ Organiser of the Birkenhead and District Society Co-operative Party. She later became a Further Education Tutor and subsequently the Co-operative Union's Sectional Education Officer in Scotland. While there she also became involved with workers' co-operatives and the setting up of the Scottish Co-operative Development Committee. She later became the Education Officer of the Co-operative Development Agency in London from where she moved to become the Education Officer of the International Co-operative Alliance. More recently she was a Lecturer in Co-operative Studies at the University of Ulster and Visiting Research Fellow at the Co-operative Research Unit at the Open University.

Dr Rhodes, who is the author of *The International Co-operative Alliance During War and Peace 1910-1950*, began her adult education as a student at the Co-operative College, Stanford Hall, Loughborough. She has chosen the College motto "Salus populi suprema est lex" to be the inscription of this study.

COOPERATIVE IDEOLOGY

MAJOR STATEMENTS

Collected By Rita Rhodes

ISBN: 9798852773722
Publisher: Rita Rhodes

British Library Cataloguing-in-Publication Data a catalogue record for this book is available on request from the British Library.

Typeset by Chris Waite of CW Services and Amazon Kindle Direct Publishing.

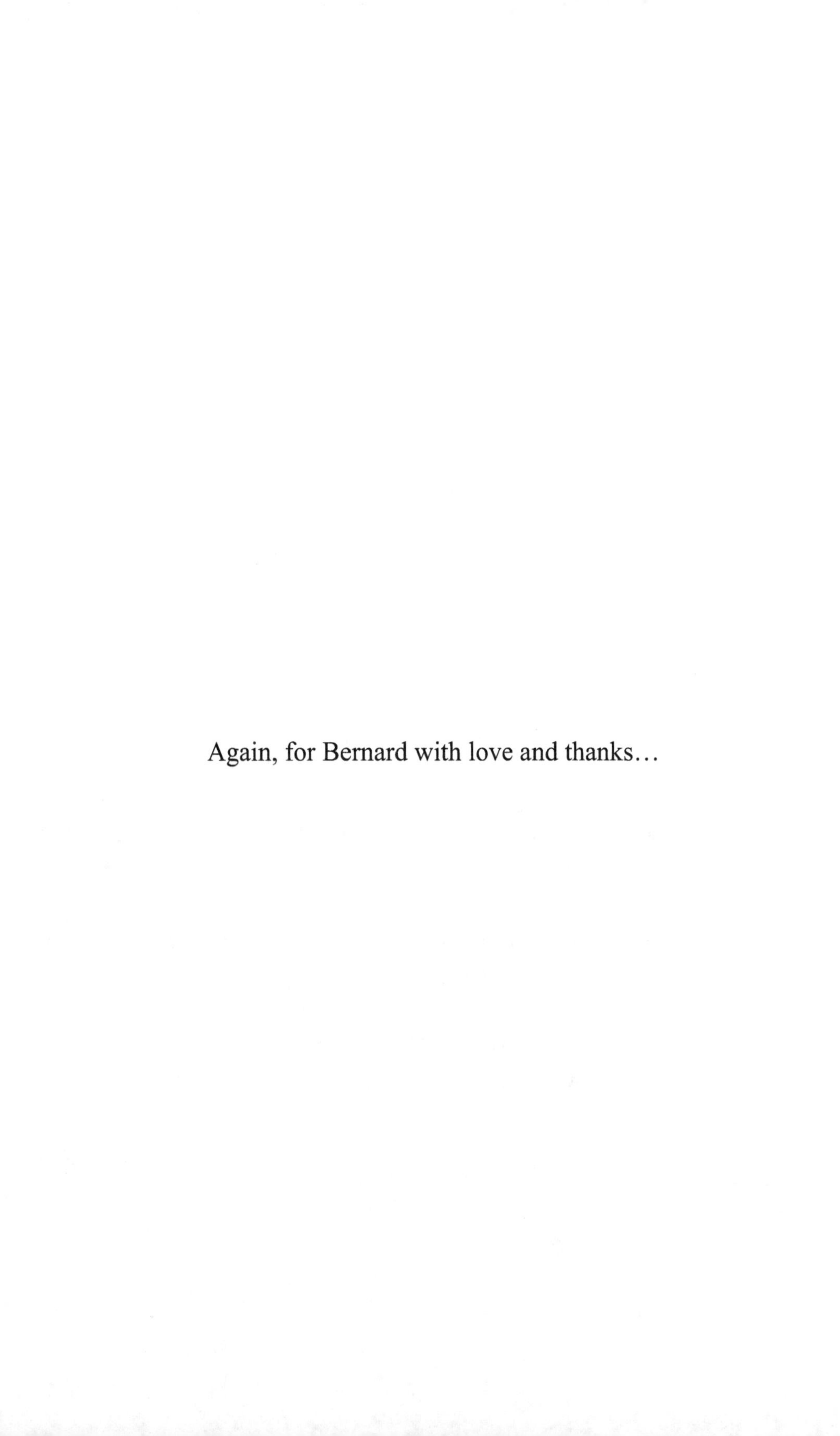

Again, for Bernard with love and thanks…

Rita Rhodes has also written:

A Thematic Guide to ICA Congresses 1895-1995 (written jointly)

The International Cooperative Alliance During War and Peace 1910 - 1950

Cooperative Adventures
We joined the Coop and Saw the World
(Joint Autobiography)

Cooperative Insights
Essays on the Political, Economic and Social Aspects of Cooperatives

Empire and Cooperation
How the British Empire Used Cooperatives in its Development Strategies 1900-1970

An Arsenal for Labour
The Royal Arsenal Co-operative Society and Politics 1896 - 1996

FOREWORD

I hope to encourage a debate on cooperative ideology, ideology being defined as a system of ideas and ideals that shape thinking and action in economic, social and political matters.

Of course balances can shift or be overtaken. It nevertheless represents distinctive beliefs shaped by the 18th century European Enlightenment and early moves from aristocracy to greater emphasis on the role of individuals within democracies. Influential also was a Labour Theory of Value epitomised in the writings of David Ricardo (1772-1823) and enshrined in early cooperative ideas by Robert Owen (1771-1858) He argued that labour was the basic factor of production and gave it centrality in the Labour Bazaars and Labour notes he introduced. Early cooperators modified these to offer higher returns to those they employed often in the form of a double dividend.

Community was a further element in cooperative thought taken to the point of establishing cooperative communities, strongly supported by Robert Owen who lost personal wealth in attempting to establish several. Reasons for failure have been well analysed but early retail societies including the Rochdale Pioneers kept them in mind, but in a changed setting. Factory production encourage population shifts into urban settings but Rochdale and others in its model saw themselves as 'communities' although in streets rather than enclosed communities. Over time they developed 'cradle to grave' provisions. Important among these were various kinds of education including classes and reading rooms. Similar facilities were being encouraged by Mechanics' Institutes and a little later by the Workers' Education Association (WEA).

Other kinds of cooperative appeared in the 19th century including Thrift and Credit Societies, People's Banks and various forms of agriculture cooperative. People's Banks started to assist early housing cooperative's . Workers' or producer cooperatives also appeared but were to have a more chequered history with tensions between them and retail societies that also developed productive capabilities.

Practical cooperative development in 19th century had ideological roots articulated by many notable cooperators. They are recalled in this volume for two main reasons. Some are being down played including member primacy and with that democracy and accountability. Just as factory production and urbanisation changed settings so are today's technological and cyber advances offering new forms and mechanisms for cooperatives. These may well prompt new ideological elements.

Historic ideological statements are given their own page(s) together with author and brief accompanying information. Hopefully readers can pick and choose which to read and think upon. Above all I hope they remind us that Cooperation is an ideology which should help make clear our different form of economic, political and social enterprises.

Contents

ROCHDALE PIONEERS

Almanac 1860

'They aimed 'by a common bond, namely that of self interest, to join together the means, the energies and the talents of all for the common benefit of each.'

Self interest was not selfishness.
It was redeemed through mutual trade.
A shared and clearly identified need was required by members.

PEACE

Cooperative Neutrality during World War I

Peace became an ideological component in early 20th century ICA passed first peace resolution 1902 it Campaigned for mediation and arbitration in international disputes.

'Heinrich Kaufmann, German Co-operative leader urged that he and his co-operative friends should try to end the war by advocating 'CO-OPERATIVE NEUTRALITY. 'So do we wish the former friendly relations between cooperative organisations shall be restored in order that we may be able to take up again our work for the promotion of co-operative ideals.' These sentiments warmly received by co-operators at a meeting in London where Sir William Maxwell, President of the ICA not only expressed warm appreciation of this message but asked for a similar message 'of our sentiment' to be sent to Mr. Kaufmann.'

Cooperative leaders in Britain, France, Germany, Holland Switzerland kept in touch with each other, often indirectly during the war. They saw it as one between capitalists and imperialists, not cooperators.

TENSION BETWEEN CONSUMER & PRODUCER COOPERATIVES

These can be illustrated by the two competing statements.

Prof Charles Gide (1847-1932)

'The programme of the consumers' societies admits capitalism to a certain extent as they are societies with shares, and as they demand from the members contributions to capital and pay them an interest and it does not admit the expropriation, properly so called of the possessing class or at least it desires a different expropriation from that which would be brought about by the play of free competition if someday the co-operative enterprises show themselves superior to capital enterprises and get rid of them by their successful development. But these are not the characteristics of collectivist expropriation and, above all, there is this difference, that the essential article of the Socialist programme, which is the class conflict, cannot be included in the co-operative programme for the obvious reason that the consumer does not represent any class; he has neither difference of class nor difference of sex: everybody is a consumer... everybody, Socialist or otherwise, has the right of admission to the association and that is a feature which suffices to give the co-operative movement its right of autonomy.'

Horace Plunkett (1854-1932) Irish Producer Cooperative – Irish Creameries

'Plunkett and Anderson were on their feet immediately, expressing amazement and indignation. Plunkett made an impassioned plea to be allowed to teach co-operation to the Irish farmer. Dairying was the one fruitful avenue open to him. Only through self-help and personal participation could the Irish farmer come to anything. He was an indifferent producer of home-made butter. Where there were proprietary creameries in Ireland, the farmer was a supplier of indifferent milk. Only by taking business and responsibility into his own hands and seeing the benefits of co-operation, could the Irish farmer acquire the qualities of mind and heart, the habits of thrift and industry that would raise him from serfdom. Paternalism, however, generous, could not uplift him now; as a policy, it would be no more successful than the coercive treatment which in the past had sought to make him a docile and useful slave.'

Bolger, Irish Cooperative Movement

THRIFT & CREDIT UNIONS FUNDING COOPERATIVE HOUSING

Henry Wolf (1840-1930)

'The experience of France, Belgium, and on the largest scale, Germany, has shown that out and out the best bodies to be entrusted with public money for the purpose of setting up working men's dwellings are co-operative societies. They produce a better and also a cheaper article. The experience of Germany shows that an advance of two-thirds of the value of a house corresponds, in fact, in the case of co-operative societies, to three-fourths of the actual cost. And dwellings set up by co-operative societies are always occupied. And co-operative societies also are found to provide so much better security that actually 97 per cent of the value of buildings have been advanced to them and never a loss has been made.'

COOPERATIVE SECTOR

THE IDEAS OF GEORGES FAUQUET (1883-1953)

George Fauquet is notable for two main reasons. One was that he served as the first head of the Cooperative Branch of the International Labour Organisation between 1922 and 1932. He was therefore influential and with close relations to the International Cooperative Alliance.

The second reason was that he was an acknowledged cooperative theorist. His leading publication was his book entitled 'The Cooperative Sector'. In it he argued that cooperatives became a distinct sector within national and international economies. The other sectors were shareholding private enterprise, state owned businesses and those that were mixed. In effect he was delineating and placing cooperatives within a distinct location. This cut across the wider and more generally held view that they comprised the Cooperative Commonwealth.

Georges Fauquet: ' The Cooperative Sector'

EXPORTING COOPERATIVES TO THE BRITISH EMPIRE

Cooperatives appeared spontaneously throughout the world but the British Empire formally encouraged them within its development programmes. Later it saw them as a means to help equip territories for independence. Participatory democratic skills wore then be required alongside those of business and organisation. Developing these became the remit of officers of the Indian and Colonial Civil Services. They were not traditional cooperators or from those they would try to equip. Rather surprisingly they learned quickly and enthusiastically. Their writings therefore add to Cooperative Ideology.

(1) H. CALVERT (Indian Civil Service)

Calvert (1875-1961)

'As all [members] lacked a sufficiency of capital, capital could not be the basis of association. The only other basis was the human individual, and accordingly the first principle of co-operation is that the members join as human persons and not as capitalists. The second principle follows from the first: for if all persons meet to satisfy the common need, there should be no distinction between them in the satisfaction of this need. They must meet on a basis of equality. The third principle is not peculiar to co-operation, but its importance in the life of a society is so very great that it deserves a special place. The act of association must be voluntary. The fourth principle is that the members join to promote the economic interests of themselves, and not of anybody else.'

Calvert's book 'The Law and Principles of Co-operation' which ran to five editions.

(2)   C.A.F.STRICKLAND   (Colonial   Civil Service)

C.A.F.STRICKLAND (1881-1962)

'People who have no cattle will not be particularly interested in co-operative dairying. That is why it would be a mistake to entrust co-operative dairying to the village autonomy, which must devote its fullest capacity to really common interests.'

Cooperation for Africa.

AFTERTHOUGHTS

An ideology is a collection of ideas and ideals that form a cohesive system of morality, economy and society. The collected statements that follow point to Cooperation comprising a distinct ideology, something far larger than a form of business with purpose and moral reasons.

The quotation of Heinrich Kaufmann highlights cooperative's pursuit of peace. That brings to mind the Maria Montesorri's view of the role of education in creating minds for peace. She observed that all too often education cultivates success through competition rather than cooperation but competition can lead to war whereas cooperation does not.

I quote statements that have hit me during my researches into Cooperative history, particularly that for my book 'The International Cooperative Alliance during War and Peace 1910-1950' and 'Empire and Cooperation 1900-1960'. The first explored how and why the ICA survived both World Wars and the Cold War when organisations with which it had close affinity and which also espoused world peace and the international brotherhood of man split under the pressures of total war. The second explored the British Empire's use of cooperatives in its economic and social development programmes when their ideologies were diametrically opposed. Nevertheless benefits were achieved for both.

Different readers will have different afterthoughts. Mine ended on testing how effective each of these ideological statements had proven. The Rochdale Pioneers provided a formula for success benefiting millions in the success of consumer cooperatives for the next century.

Prof. Charles Gide developed accompanying economic theory to these which also distinguished cooperation from other forms of socialism. Whereas some other socialist forms favoured revolution cooperatives were evolutionary. They competed with the aim of dominating a market which many did eventually and for a very long time.

It is more difficult to assess the impact of Henry Wolff because his influence stemmed from his extensive writings in books, articles and submissions to government, especially those governing India and Ireland. Among cooperative audiences he argued pre Keynes' theory of multiplicity, that surpluses created new income which could even support other kinds of cooperative. The ones he directly quoted were housing cooperatives facilitated by thrift and credit societies. This had potential for Cooperative development which it can be argued has been under-employed.

This takes us onto the idea of the Cooperative Sector propounded by Georges Fauquet. I personally warmed to this in teaching Social Economics in Scottish Further Education when I took students through the elements of Britain's mixed economy. This tended to overlook tensions between retail societies and workers' cooperatives as highlighted by Sir Horace Plunkett in Coop Union Congress exchanges. Apart from these tensions it is perhaps difficult to personalise the influence of Georges Fauquet because of his leadership of and consequently close identification with the Cooperative Branch of the International Labour Organisation. However his book 'Cooperative Sector' is considered a classic in Cooperative literature and joins the celebrated writings of Henry Wolff.

Sir Horace Plunkett is the Cooperative progenitor for whom I have come to have the highest regard. He was a staunch cooperator but sought to influence anyone irrespective of race, status or religious faith. That says much for a pioneer developing cooperatives in Ireland. He was a pragmatist and whereas some kinds of cooperative, particularly the retail in Britain sought independence from government, Plunkett recognised governments could assist early cooperative development in appropriate legislation and provision of training facilities. Moreover Plunkett was a major developer of cooperative support organisations that were non-governmental. His Irish Agricultural Organisation Society was replicated in Scotland, England and Wales but his Plunkett Foundation established in 1919 and sited in London was the most influential. It included the Cooperative Library which he had founded earlier in Dublin arguing that successful cooperative development required exchanges of experiences. It became the basis of the Foundation's considerable research and training capacities. Plunkett's entree to governments was assisted by his being part of the aristocratic Anglo Irish family but this was soon augmented by British government and those in its imperial territories wanting to learn more as t how cooperatives could aid farming. In response the Plunkett Foundation was soon advising on appropriate cooperative legislation and devising training programmes to prepare implementation. Alongside of this training manuals were also prepared and distributed.

The Plunkett Foundation was a seminal influence with members of the Indian and Colonial Civil Services. Members had periodic home leave during which they could join training programmes that the foundation organised for them, compounding legislative advice to the British government and those of their own territories and the training programmes Plunkett organised in those territories.

Calvert and Strickland learned much from Plunkett home leave training programmes. The final thought is though what effect did they and sympathetic colleagues have? Well the answer is that they took cooperation throughout the British Empire. As a result I hold it became history's largest developer of cooperatives. Of course independence brought change followed by evolution.

Nevertheless my final thought is that Cooperation has an ideology. It has a number of elements that past cooperative theorists have given us down the years. One not recalled was the statement of Heinrich Kaufmann, the German cooperative leader during WW1 on cooperatives as propounders of peace. That became entrenched in international Co-operative policy but surely needs restating today loud and clear. War, climate catastrophe, pestilence and capitalist corrupt governments need to be replaced by fraternity, mutuality, equality, democracy and accountability. These add up to Co-operative Ideology.